Quinoa Recipes For Weight Loss

Health and Weight Loss Recipes

Sarah Clarence

© 2012 by Sarah Clarence
ISBN-13: 978-1470114725
ISBN-10: 1470114720

All Rights Reserved.

All Rights Reserved. No part of this publication may be reproduced in any form or by any means, including scanning, photocopying, or otherwise without prior written permission of the copyright holder.

Second Printing, 2012

Printed in the United States of America

Disclaimer/Legal Notice
The information presented represents the view of the author as of the day of publication. Due to the rate at which conditions change, the author reserves the right to alter and update her opinions based on new conditions.

This book is for informational and entertainment purposes only. The author is not a doctor, nor a nutritionist and is writing simply based on her experience. While every attempt was made to accurately state the information provided here, neither the author nor her affiliates or publisher assume any responsibility for errors, inaccuracies or omissions.

Please consult your doctor before starting any new diet or exercise program.

Quinoa Recipes For Weight Loss

Health and Weight Loss Recipes

Other Books By Sarah Clarence

Baking With Quinoa: Healthier Bread, Muffin, Cookie and Cake Recipes

Table of Contents

Introduction 7
   The Three Most Popular Quinoa Varieties 8
   The Health Benefits of Quinoa 9
   How Quinoa Compares to Rice 9
   Quinoa For Weight Loss 10
   How to Cook and Eat Quinoa 11

Quinoa Recipes 13
   Breakfast Recipes 13
     Start the Morning Off Right Quinoa 13
     Morning Blueberry Quinoa 14
     Easy and Healthy Quinoa Breakfast 14
     Pecan and Cinnamon Quinoa 15
     Sweet Quinoa with Fruit 16
   Bread Recipes 17
     Tasty Cornbread With Quinoa 17
     Zucchini and Quinoa Bread 18
     Crispy Quinoa Crackers 19
     Quinoa Banana Muffins 20
     Hearty Quinoa Bread 21
   Quinoa and Vegetables Recipes 23
     Spicy Vegetable Quinoa 23
     Quinoa with Spinach 24
     Spicy Carrot Quinoa 25
     Easy Quinoa Cauliflower 26
   Quinoa Salad Recipes 29
     Cold Quinoa Salad 29
     Fresh and Light Summer Salad 30
     Green Bean Quinoa Salad 31
     Mango Salad with Quinoa 32
     Sweet and Spicy Quinoa Salad 33
     Spicy Quinoa Salad 34

Quinoa Main Courses 37
Meat-Free Quinoa Meat Loaf 37
Quinoa Spicy Burgers 38
Baked Spinach Quinoa Loaf.................................. 39
Quinoa Veggie Stew 40
Feta Cheese and Quinoa Patties 41

Quinoa Treats and Desserts 43
Coconut and Blueberry Quinoa Pudding 43
Fruit and Quinoa Yogurt Treat 44
Cranberry and Cherry Quinoa Pudding 44
Creamy Peanut Butter Cookies.............................. 45
Honey Apple Quinoa 46

Conclusion.. 49

Introduction

Quinoa, pronounced keen-wah, is said to be a powerhouse of nutrition, flavor and texture. Can it really be all that? When it comes to losing weight, keeping it off and feeling great, yes, quinoa can be all that.

Although many think of quinoa as a grain, it is actually a seed of a plant in the same family as beets, chard, and spinach. Before you say 'yuck' and close this book for good, just read on and try at least one of the delicious recipes that follow. You will become a convert to this very versatile grain-like food, I'm certain.

The Three Most Popular Quinoa Varieties

There are many types of quinoa, but there are three main types of quinoa sold commercially. They are gold, red and black. Each one is unique from the others.

Gold Quinoa
The most common variety of quinoa is gold. You should be able to find this variety more easily than the other two. The gold quinoa is fluffier, lighter, and creamier than either red or black quinoa. It also has a texture that mixes well with many foods and is easily incorporated into baked goods. It can also be used as a good substitute for hot oatmeal as it mixes well with milk. If you haven't yet tried quinoa, trying the gold variety is a good place to start.

Red Quinoa
Red quinoa has a bitter taste and is crunchier than the gold. Red quinoa is higher in protein, calories and fiber than gold quinoa. Because of the red coloring, using this quinoa makes your dishes look vibrant and colorful. Due to its bitter flavor, red quinoa is often used in dishes such as butternut squash and avocado to make a savory combination of flavors. It is also a great treat on top of a salad.

Black Quinoa
Black quinoa is not produced in large quantities so it can be difficult to find. Black quinoa is sweeter than gold and is crispier in texture than either the red or the gold. If you can find black quinoa it is fun to experiment with various dishes to see how its unique taste brings out the flavor of other foods.

The Health Benefits of Quinoa

There are so many health benefits to quinoa that this topic alone could fill a book or two. That is why, if you haven't tried it yet, you should. Quinoa is a complete protein, containing all nine essential amino acids. In addition, just one cup of quinoa contains about 200 calories, 40 grams of carbohydrates, 8 grams of protein, 3.5 grams of fat, and 5 grams of fiber. If you are a vegetarian, this is an excellent way to get both all of the essential amino acids in your diet, and it is also a good source of protein.

Quinoa is also a good source of phosphorus, manganese, magnesium, and lysine, which is essential for tissue growth and repair. It is also believed that quinoa can be helpful for those people who suffer from diabetes, and atherosclerosis. Additionally, quinoa is a good source of magnesium, which is a mineral that helps to relax blood vessels, which can help reduce the frequency and severity of migraines.

And finally, one of the most highly valued aspects of quinoa for many people is that quinoa by itself contains no gluten or wheat. However, if you want to make leavened baked treats, it needs to be combined with wheat flour (which some of the recipes below contain). Quinoa flour is available and it can be used to make pasta. You can also buy quinoa pasta.

How Quinoa Compares to Rice

Quinoa fares better than brown and white rice in several ways. Quinoa is higher in vitamin B2, calcium, iron potassium, zinc and magnesium than either brown or white rice. It is still not widely available in most grocery stores, but it can be found online or in most health food stores.

Although quinoa tends to be more expensive than rice, one cup of quinoa cooks up to about 3 cups cooked, so the cost difference is not as great as one might initially believe.

Quinoa For Weight Loss

One of the biggest hurdles to over come when trying to lose weight is the feeling of always being hungry. If you have suffered from this problem, then quinoa may be the solution you have been looking for. Quinoa is rich in both protein and fiber. This means that you are more likely to feel full while still maintaining weight loss goals.

Quinoa also doesn't cause a sharp jump in blood sugar. Eating foods such as quinoa, (which is on the low glycemic index) means that you will be less likely to crave bread and sweets. Slow and steady blood sugar levels are important for many reasons, and quinoa will help you get there.

Quinoa is also low in calories. One serving of quinoa is quite a lot of quinoa and only contains about 200 calories. You could eat several servings of quinoa and still have fewer calories than one serving of pasta. Quinoa is so versatile, it can be substituted for almost any grain in almost any recipe.

For all of these reasons, quinoa may be the perfect food to add to your diet if you are trying to lose weight. Because of the high amounts of protein and fiber, as well as the low glycemic index and low calories, you will feel full which will help you reach your healthy weight loss goals.

How to Cook and Eat Quinoa

It can be a good idea to rinse quinoa seeds with water prior to cooking. This is because the quinoa seeds have a natural coating that has a bitter taste. Commercial processes remove much of this residue, but it is still a good idea to rinse the seeds in cold water, until the water runs clear, to make sure the process is complete.

In any quinoa recipe, it will either call for dry quinoa or cooked quinoa. Quinoa, like rice, cooks up to a greater volume. So, one cup *cooked quinoa* is different from one cup *dry quinoa, cooked*. One-fourth cup of dry quinoa cooks up to about 1 cup of cooked quinoa. So, in a recipe that calls for 2 cups cooked quinoa, you will cook 1/2 cup of uncooked quinoa to yield the two cups of cooked quinoa that you need.

To cook the quinoa, after rinsing the seeds, bring a pot of one part quinoa and two parts water to a boil. Then cover the pot and simmer for fifteen minutes. When you see the sprouts popping out, you'll know the quinoa is just about ready. At this point, stir the quinoa so all the water gets absorbed.

Alternatively, you can dry roast the seeds before cooking them. This will keep more of the natural nutty flavor.

Quinoa by itself can taste quite bland. But the good news is that you can add just about anything to it to spice it up and make it a delicious and nutritious breakfast, lunch, dinner or snack! Once you have prepared the quinoa, there are so many ways that you can use these seeds in cooking. You can use quinoa in hot or cold dishes. You can put it into a salad or in a soup. You can mix it in with meat patties. You can also add quinoa to your favorite pancake, waffle or muffin batter. You will see that once you start using quinoa, it will become a regular ingredient in so many of the dishes that you prepare.

It is important to store dry quinoa in a tightly sealed container and place it in a cool, dry place. Uneaten cooked quinoa should be stored in an airtight container and placed in the refrigerator.

Using quinoa is an easy way to give your nutrition a real boost. The recipes in this book are only a start. With a little imagination you can easily create a new quinoa creation every day, and you will be feeling healthier and looking leaner in no time!

Quinoa Recipes

Breakfast Recipes

Quinoa is an excellent way to incorporate good nutrition and high protein into your breakfast. You can cook the quinoa ahead of time to make breakfast preparation quick.

Start the Morning Off Right Quinoa

Ingredients
1/2 cup dry quinoa
1 1/2 cups rice milk
1 cup chopped apricots
1/4 teaspoon vanilla extract
2 tablespoons golden raisins

Directions
Note: Rinse the quinoa seeds with water until water runs clear, prior to cooking.
In a medium saucepan over low heat, combine quinoa and rice milk. Cover and cook for fifteen minutes until quinoa is tender. Stir in vanilla, raisins and apricots.

Transfer 2 cups of the quinoa mixture to a blender and blend.

Mix blended quinoa with the rest. Serve immediately warm. Makes 6 (1/2 cup) servings.

Morning Blueberry Quinoa
This is so tasty it is easily my family's favorite!

Ingredients
2 cups milk
1 cup dry quinoa
3 tablespoons brown sugar
1/8 teaspoon ground cinnamon
1 cup blueberries (fresh is best, but frozen, thawed, will work as well)

Directions
Note: Rinse the quinoa seeds with water until water runs clear, prior to cooking.
In a small saucepan over medium heat, bring milk just to a boil, then add quinoa and return just to a boil.

Reduce heat to low and cover. Simmer about 15 minutes, until most of the milk has been absorbed.

Slowly stir in cinnamon and sugar. Cover again and cook an additional 8 minutes, or until most of the remaining milk has been absorbed.

Stir in blueberries and cook a few seconds more.

Serve with additional cinnamon, sugar, milk, and blueberries as desired. Makes 6 (1/2 cup) servings.

Easy and Healthy Quinoa Breakfast
This quinoa breakfast will keep you full all morning long!

Ingredients
1 cup cooked quinoa (see **How to Cook Quinoa** section if you have not cooked quinoa before.)
1 cup soymilk

2 tablespoons chopped walnuts
2 tablespoons raisins
2 tablespoons chopped figs
1/4 teaspoon salt
1/2 teaspoon cinnamon

Directions
Note: Rinse the quinoa seeds with water until water runs clear, prior to cooking.

In a medium-sized pan, on medium heat, mix all ingredients together.

Stir until the liquid as evaporated.

Add more milk to your liking. Makes 2 servings.

Pecan and Cinnamon Quinoa

Ingredients
1 cup low fat milk
1 cup water
1/2 teaspoon cinnamon
1/3 cup chopped pecans, lightly roasted
1 cup quinoa (gold or red quinoa are both excellent choices)
2 cups fresh blackberries

Directions
Note: Rinse the quinoa seeds with water until water runs clear, prior to cooking.
In a medium saucepan over medium heat, combine quinoa, water, and milk. Bring to boil.

Reduce heat, cover, and simmer over low heat for fifteen minutes, until most of the liquid is absorbed.

In a small skillet on medium heat, roast the pecans for three minutes.

Remove the quinoa from heat and let stand covered for five minutes.

To the quinoa, stir in cinnamon and blackberries. Place in four bowls and top with roasted pecans.

Makes four servings.

Sweet Quinoa with Fruit
This is a quick and easy breakfast or snack. If you have the quinoa made ahead of time, it can be even quicker!

Ingredients
2/3 cup cooked quinoa (see **How to Cook Quinoa** section if you have not cooked quinoa before.)
1/3 cup unsweetened almond milk
Maple syrup or brown sugar to taste
Toppings of your choice: raisins, pistachios, cinnamon, walnuts, or peaches are good choices.

Directions
In a medium-size pan, on low heat, combine cooked quinoa and milk until warmed through.

Sweeten to taste with maple syrup. Add desired toppings.

Makes 1 serving.

Bread Recipes

Quinoa breads and muffins are made with quinoa flour. Quinoa flour on its own can have a grassy taste. To help eliminate that and to provide 'rise' for breads, you need to add wheat flour. If you choose to not use wheat flour along with quinoa flour in recipes that you create, you will want to place the quinoa flour on a baking sheet, spread evenly about 1/4 inch thick, and place in a 215 degree (F.) oven for about two hours. This will eliminate the grassy taste. Even quinoa flour that says it is 'pre-toasted' may need to be toasted again.

Tasty Cornbread With Quinoa

Ingredients
1 tablespoon butter, to grease pan
1 cup whole wheat flour
3/4 cup yellow cornmeal
1 teaspoon baking powder
1/2 teaspoon baking soda
1/2 teaspoon dried mixed herbs (your choice)
2 eggs
1 1/2 cups cooked quinoa, cooled (see **How to Cook Quinoa** section if you have not cooked quinoa before.)
3 tablespoons unsalted butter, melted and cooled
3 tablespoons brown sugar
3/4 teaspoon salt
2 cups milk
1 1/2 tablespoons white wine vinegar
1 cup heavy cream

Directions
Note: Rinse the quinoa seeds with water until water runs clear, prior to cooking.

Preheat an oven to 350 degrees (F).

Butter a 10-inch baking dish.

In a large bowl, mix together cornmeal, flour, baking soda, baking powder, and dried herbs.

In a medium-sized bowl, beat eggs and add melted butter, and quinoa. Mix well. Then stir in salt, vinegar, sugar, and milk.

Slowly add the wet ingredients to the dry ingredients and mix. Batter will be thin.

Pour batter into baking dish.

Pour cream into the middle of the batter. Do not stir mixture.

Place in the oven and bake 45 minutes.

Cornbread is done when the top is light brown.

Zucchini and Quinoa Bread

Ingredients
2/3 cup melted coconut oil
1 1/2 cups sugar
2 cups zucchini, grated
1 cup quinoa flour
1 cup whole wheat flour
3 eggs
1 teaspoon baking powder
1/4 teaspoon baking soda
1 teaspoon salt
1 teaspoon pure vanilla
1 tablespoon cinnamon

Directions
Preheat oven to 350 degrees (F).

Grease and flour two large bread tins. Set aside.

In a large bowl with an electric mixer beat together the coconut oil, eggs, and sugar.

Put in the remaining ingredients and mix together.

Spoon half of the mixture into each bread tins.

Sprinkle a bit of sugar on top of each loaf.

Bake for 45 minutes, or until the center of each loaf springs back when lightly touched.

Crispy Quinoa Crackers

Ingredients
1 1/2 cups white flour
1/2 cup oat bran
2 teaspoons baking powder
1/4 cup powdered milk
2 tbsp shortening
1 teaspoon salt
1 cup malted barley
1/2 cup quinoa flour
1/2 cup warm water

Directions
Preheat oven to 400 degrees (F).

In a large bowl, mix shortening into all dry ingredients.

Add water and stir well.

Lightly flour surface and knead dough for five minutes. Cut into 4 parts.

Roll each piece thin and cut into desired shapes. Use cookie cutters for fancier crackers.

Bake for until light brown (about 5-6 minutes). Cool and store uneaten crackers into an airtight container.

Quinoa Banana Muffins

My family enjoys these muffins and I make banana, blueberry and apple regularly so that everyone eventually gets their favorite.

Ingredients
2 eggs
1/2 cup quinoa flour
1/2 cup wheat flour
1/3 cup brown sugar
2 tablespoons honey
2 teaspoons baking powder
1 teaspoon baking soda
1/2 teaspoon salt
2 ripe bananas (you can also use fresh blueberries or grated apple if you prefer)

Directions
Preheat oven to 400 degrees (F).

In a large bowl, mix flour, flakes and all dry ingredients.

Mix in mashed bananas and all wet ingredients.

Pour into greased muffin tins, filling tins about 1/2 full.

Bake 20 minutes or until lightly brown and knife stuck in center comes out clean.

Makes 12 muffins.

Hearty Quinoa Bread
This is a rich tasting bread that we have almost every week. You can find quinoa flour online.

Ingredients
1 cup brown rice flour
1/2 cup quinoa flour
1/2 cup cornstarch
1/3 cup sweet rice flour
3/4 cup gluten free oat flour
3 tablespoons brown sugar
1 tablespoon flax seeds with 2 tablespoon of boiling water
3 eggs
1 1/2 teaspoon salt
1 tablespoon molasses
1 teaspoon apple cider vinegar
4 tablespoon butter or margarine, melted
1 packet active dry yeast PLUS 1 teaspoon granulated sugar (for proofing yeast)
1/4 cup plus 1 cup heated water (around 120 degrees F)

Directions
Grease the bottoms of two 8-inch bread pans

Preheat oven to 200 degrees then turn oven off.

In a medium-sized bowl, sift together dry ingredients.

In a small bowl, combine the molasses, vinegar, eggs, and melted butter.

In a small bowl, stir together yeast and one teaspoon of sugar in a small bowl. To this add 1/4 cup of heated (warm, not boiling) water.

Let this yeast mixture stand for 10 minutes. (If it is not foamy and active after ten minutes then start over with another packet of yeast.)

Once the yeast is ready, add egg mixture to the dry ingredients, and add the yeast mixture.

With a mixer, beat this dough mixture on high for about 15 minutes. Slowly adding the remaining cup of warm water. Batter should be stiff.

If the dough is too runny, add a little more rice flour to achieve the right dough consistency.

Divide dough in half and place in greased 8-inch pans. Place pans in warm oven to rise for 60 to 90 minutes. You can place a towel over the pan.

When dough rises to the top of the pan, bake bread for 40 minutes at 350 degrees (F) or until a thermometer placed in the center of each loaf reads 190 degrees (F).

Yields two small loaves of bread.

Quinoa and Vegetables Recipes

Don't eat enough vegetables? Adding quinoa to your vegetables will add both extra flavor and texture that you will love!

Spicy Vegetable Quinoa

Ingredients
1/2 teaspoon salt
1/4 teaspoon red pepper
1/4 teaspoon black pepper
1 cup dry quinoa
2 cloves minced garlic
1/2 teaspoon thyme
1/4 teaspoon marjoram
2 medium sliced sweet potatoes
1 peeled eggplant, cut into cubes
1 medium-size tomato, wedged
1 sliced green bell pepper
1 small sweet onion, wedged
2 cups low-sodium chicken broth
Non-stick cooking spray

Directions
Preheat oven to 450°(F).

Line a large cookie sheet or jelly-roll pan with foil and coat with cooking spray.

Place the eggplant, bell pepper, tomato, potatoes, and onion on the pan. Spray the vegetables lightly with more cooking spray. Sprinkle black pepper, ground red pepper, and salt over vegetables.

Bake for 20 minutes or until vegetables are tender and browned.

Rinse the quinoa in water until the water runs clear.

In a medium-sized saucepan, coat with cooking spray and stir together garlic, marjoram and thyme on low heat for 1 to 2 minutes.

Add quinoa and cook for an additional 2 to 3 minutes.

Increase heat to high and add water or broth and bring to a boil. Reduce heat to low.

Cover and simmer until water is absorbed, about 15 minutes.

Place vegetables in a large bowl and fold in quinoa. Serve immediately. Serves 6.

Quinoa with Spinach
This spinach dish makes an excellent side or main dish. It is also nutrient rich, and, of course, delicious!

Ingredients
1 tablespoon olive oil
2 cloves fresh garlic, minced
1 medium leek, sliced thin
1/3 cup golden raisins
2 cups baby spinach leaves
2 cups reduced-sodium chicken or vegetable broth
2 cups butternut squash, peeled and diced
1 cup dry quinoa
2 tablespoons walnuts, chopped

Directions
Note: Rinse the quinoa seeds with water until water runs clear, prior to cooking.

In a large saucepan over medium heat, heat the oil.

To the oil, add the garlic and leeks. Stir while cooking, about 5 minutes until leeks are soft.

Add the squash, quinoa, broth, and raisins. Bring mixture to a boil.

Reduce the heat and cover. Simmer about fifteen minutes or until all liquid is absorbed. Quinoa and squash should be tender.

Slowly stir in spinach and cook until leaves begin to wilt, about 2 minutes.

Remove from heat and sprinkle with walnuts. Serve immediately.

Makes 4 servings.

Spicy Carrot Quinoa
This is a very easy vegetable side dish! I serve this with many of my favorite chicken dishes. It is also filling enough to have as a main dish of its own.

Instructions
2 tablespoons olive oil
1 tablespoon fresh garlic, minced
1 pinch cayenne powder
1/2 teaspoon cumin
2 cups peeled baby carrots, chopped
1 14-oz can garbanzo beans, drained and rinsed
2 cups reduced-sodium vegetable or chicken broth
1 cup dry quinoa
1/4 cup chopped parsley
dash of salt and pepper

Directions
Note: Rinse the quinoa seeds with water until water runs clear, prior to cooking.

In a large saucepan, over medium heat, heat oil.

Lower the heat and to the oil, add the garlic, cayenne powder, and cumin. Stir for about 30 seconds.

To the oil mixture, add the garbanzo beans, carrots, and broth. Increase the heat to medium and bring the mixture to boil.

Add quinoa and cover and simmer for 30 minutes. All liquid will be absorbed.

Stir in parsley and season with salt and pepper as desired.

Makes 6 servings.

Easy Quinoa Cauliflower
If you are not a cauliflower fan, give this recipe a try. It just may convert you!

Ingredients
1 cup chopped sweet onion
1 tablespoon olive oil
2 cups dry quinoa
1/2 teaspoon salt
4 cups chopped fresh cauliflower
5 cups water (or vegetable broth if you prefer)

Directions
Note: Rinse the quinoa seeds with water until water runs clear, prior to cooking.

In large pot, on medium heat, stir in onion and oil and cook for about 1 minute.

To the oil mixture, add quinoa. Cook and stir for 5 minutes.

To the quinoa, add salt, cauliflower, and 4 cups water. Stir and bring to a boil.

Reduce heat to low and cover pot.

Simmer until all water has absorbed.

Remove from heat. With a potato masher, mash mixture together.

If necessary, add a little water to create a creamy consistency.

Yields 8 servings.

Quinoa Salad Recipes

Adding good nutrition can easily be done by adding quinoa to your favorite salads. For something new and tasty, the following salads may become your new favorites!

Cold Quinoa Salad

Ingredients for the Salad
1 cup dry quinoa
9 ounces green beans (cut off tops and tails, then cut in narrow diagonal strips)
10 1/2 ounces cherry tomatoes (wash tomatoes and cut in quarters)
7 ounces feta cheese
Handful of pumpkin seeds (toast in a dry skillet for a minute)
black olives, chopped

Ingredients for the Dressing
juice from one medium-sized lemon
1 1/2 tablespoon balsamic or red wine vinegar
2 tablespoons olive oil
dash of salt and black pepper

Directions
Note: Rinse the quinoa seeds with water until water runs clear, prior to cooking.

In a medium-sized skillet over low heat, brown quinoa until it starts to change color.

Stir in three cups hot water and a pinch of salt.

Simmer for 10 minutes or until quinoa tender.

Add beans. Cover pan and simmer until water is completely absorbed.

Remove from heat and allow to cool.

To make the dressing, mix lemon juice, oil, and balsamic or red wine vinegar together. Add black pepper and salt. Set aside.

Add olives, tomatoes, the pumpkin seeds to the quinoa and beans.
Drizzle dressing over this mixture and crumble in the feta cheese.

Serve immediately.

Makes 4 servings.

Fresh and Light Summer Salad
This salad is a staple in our house during the summer. It is tasty as well as filling.

Salad Ingredients
1 cup dry quinoa
2 cups water
1/2 of a red onion, sliced
2 whole tomatoes, chopped
1 cucumber, peeled and chopped
1/2 cup fresh basil, chopped
1/4 cup pine nuts

Dressing Ingredients
4 garlic cloves-minced
1 1/2 teaspoons lemon juice
3 tablespoons balsamic vinegar
1/2 teaspoon crushed red pepper

1/2 teaspoon salt
1/2 teaspoon Dijon mustard
1/4 cup olive oil

Directions

Note: Rinse the quinoa seeds with water until water runs clear, prior to cooking.

In a medium-sized pot, bring water to a boil and add quinoa.

Cover and simmer over low heat for 15 minutes or until water is absorbed.

Set aside and let cool.

In a small bowl, whisk together all dressing ingredients except olive oil.

Add olive oil, a little at a time to allow oil and vinegar to mix.

Toss all salad ingredients and quinoa with dressing. Top with pine nuts.

Green Bean Quinoa Salad

Ingredients for Salad
1/2 cup black quinoa
1 pound green beans, trimmed
2 green onions
1/2 cup hazelnuts, skinned, toasted, and chopped

Ingredients for Dressing
1/4 cup olive oil
3 tablespoons white balsamic vinegar
2 teaspoons honey
1 clove fresh garlic, minced

one handful of basil leaves
dash of salt and pepper

Directions
Note: Rinse the quinoa seeds with water until water runs clear, prior to cooking.

In a blender, blend all dressing ingredients together.

Add salt and pepper and refrigerate.

Bring 1 cup water to a boil and add quinoa.

Reduce heat, cover, and simmer, for about 20 minutes or until all liquid is absorbed.

Place quinoa in a large serving bowl to cool.

Steam green beans until just soft. Drain well and add green beans to cooled quinoa.

Slice scallions thinly. Take half of the hazelnuts and scallions and add to the quinoa and beans.

Toss with dressing and top with the rest of the hazelnuts.

Makes four to six servings.

Mango Salad with Quinoa
The combination of mangos and avocados in this quinoa salad is amazing.

Ingredients
1 cup uncooked black quinoa
2 cups water
2 medium avocados, diced
1 large mango, diced
2 large tomatoes, diced

3 green onions, sliced
1/2 cup chopped cilantro
1/2 teaspoon cumin
1/4 cup fresh lime juice
1 tablespoon olive oil
dash of salt and pepper

Directions
Note: Rinse the quinoa seeds with water until water runs clear, prior to cooking.

In a medium-sized pot, bring water to a boil and add quinoa. Boil for 5 minutes.

Lower the heat and simmer for about 15 minutes, or until water is absorbed. Remove from heat and let cool.

In a large bowl, combine the quinoa, avocado, mango, tomatoes, green onions, and cilantro.

In a small bowl, whisk together the olive oil, cumin and lime juice.

Pour the dressing over the salad and mix to coat.

Season with salt and pepper. Chill before serving.

Sweet and Spicy Quinoa Salad

Ingredients
1 cup quinoa
1 can black beans, drained
1 red bell pepper, diced
1 green onion stalk, chopped fine
2 teaspoons honey
juice from 1/2 lime

2 teaspoons rice vinegar
2 teaspoons olive oil
pinch of salt

Directions
Note: Rinse the quinoa seeds with water until water runs clear, prior to cooking.

In a medium pan, boil water and add quinoa. Reduce heat, cover and simmer for twenty minutes or until water is absorbed.

In a large mixing bowl, combine the cooked quinoa with red pepper, green onion, and black beans.

In a blender or jar with a tight lid, mix rice vinegar, honey, olive oil, lime juice, and pinch of salt. Mix well.

Pour dressing over quinoa mixture and toss salad.

Serve immediately. Makes 4 servings.

Spicy Quinoa Salad
I absolutely love this dish during the summer months. It is delicious!

Ingredients
1 cup quinoa, well rinsed
2 cups water
1 large diced tomato
6 green leaf lettuce leaves, torn
1 tablespoon olive oil
1/4 cup fresh cilantro, chopped
1/8 teaspoon black pepper
1/2 teaspoon salt
1 teaspoon chili powder

3/4 cup mild chunky salsa
1 cup frozen corn, thawed
1 15-ounce can black beans, rinsed and drained
1/2 large chopped sweet onion

Directions
Note: Rinse the quinoa seeds with water until water runs clear, prior to cooking.

In a medium saucepan over high heat, bring two cups water to a boil, then stir in quinoa. Reduce heat to medium, cover and simmer ten minutes.

To the quinoa, add corn, 1/4 cup salsa, beans, salt, black pepper, and chili powder.

Increase heat to medium and bring mixture to a boil. Lower heat, cover and cook two minutes more until quinoa is soft.

Stir in oil, 1/4 cup salsa, and cilantro. Simmer until thickened.

Top lettuce leaves with quinoa mixture, onion, tomato, and remaining 1/4 cup of salsa for individual servings.

Makes 6 servings.

Quinoa Main Courses

One great thing about quinoa is its versatility. It is so easy to toss it into your favorite main dishes. Its slightly nutty flavor adds a twist to favorite dishes, and it is also a great base for creating new dishes.

Meat-Free Quinoa Meat Loaf

Adding quinoa to your favorite, or new favorite, meatloaf is both delicious and nutritious!

Ingredients
1 egg
2 tablespoons olive oil
8 ounces fresh mushrooms, sliced
1 can garbanzo beans
3/4 cup oats
2 cups cooked quinoa (see **How to Cook Quinoa** section if you have not cooked quinoa before.)
1 cup frozen green peas
1 cup sweet onions, finely chopped
10 sundried tomatoes in oil, chopped
fresh parsley
dash of salt and pepper

Directions
Preheat oven to 350 degrees (F).

Lightly grease the bottom of an 8-inch loaf pan with oil.

In a large skillet, heat oil on medium heat.

To the oil, add mushrooms, onions, and salt and pepper.

Stir until mushrooms are golden brown, about 6 minutes.

In a blender, put oats, beans, and 1/2 cup water and blend until smooth.

In a large bowl, combine mushrooms, quinoa, peas, bean and oat mixture, parsley, tomatoes, onion, egg, salt and pepper.

Pour this mixture to a loaf pan and gently press and shape evenly, with a slight rise in the middle.

Bake for 60 minutes until firm and golden brown.

Let the loaf cool for a few minutes before slicing. Serve immediately.

Quinoa Spicy Burgers
These burgers are so good, they may soon be the only kind of burgers you make.

Ingredients
2 cups cooked quinoa (see **How to Cook Quinoa** section if you have not cooked quinoa before.)
3/4 cup shredded cheddar cheese
1/2 cup low-fat cottage cheese
1 medium carrot, grated
3 eggs
3 tablespoons all purpose flour
2 green onions
1/2 teaspoon sugar
1/4 teaspoon black pepper
1/4 teaspoon ground cumin
1/8 teaspoon salt
1/8 teaspoon garlic powder
Olive oil for frying

Directions
In a large bowl combine the cooked quinoa, eggs, flour, cheddar cheese, cottage cheese, carrot, onions, sugar, cumin, and garlic powder, salt and pepper.

In a large frying pan over low heat, heat a tablespoon of olive oil.

Using a large spoon, drop mixture into pan and flatten to about 1/2 inch thick. Fry until golden-brown, about 5 minutes on each side.

Makes 10 tasty burgers.

Baked Spinach Quinoa Loaf

Ingredients
1 pound fresh spinach, washed
2 teaspoons olive oil
2 cloves fresh minced garlic
1 tablespoon fresh thyme leaves
1 teaspoon fresh rosemary, finely chopped
1 diced yellow onion
1/4 teaspoon crushed red-pepper flakes
1 cup nonfat cottage cheese
1/4 teaspoon black pepper
2 large eggs, beaten lightly
1 cup quinoa, cooked (see **How to Cook Quinoa** section if you have not cooked quinoa before.)
Olive-oil cooking spray

Directions
Preheat oven to 350 degrees (F).

With cooking spray, coat an 8 x 8 inch baking dish, and then spread breadcrumbs on the bottom.

Fill a large bowl with water and ice.

In a medium pot, boil water and place spinach for about 10 to 15 seconds. Carefully take spinach out place in the ice bowl. When spinach is cold, squeeze out all excess water. Chop into small pieces.

In a medium-sized pan, heat the olive oil and add garlic, thyme, rosemary, onion, and red-pepper flakes. Sauté until onions are clear, about 5 minutes.

In a medium-sized bowl and add quinoa, cottage cheese, pepper, spinach, and eggs to the onion mixture, and stir well.

Pour mixture into prepared baking dish and bake in the oven about 60 minutes. Loaf should be set and the edges brown.

Slice and serve immediately.

Quinoa Veggie Stew

My family loves this stew during the cold winter months. It is filling and delicious.

Ingredients
1 finely chopped sweet onion
1 red bell pepper, cut in half-inch pieces
2 teaspoons olive oil
1 tablespoon paprika
2 teaspoons coriander
1 1/2 teaspoon cumin
6 cups low-sodium vegetable broth
1 pound red potatoes, cut into half-inch pieces
1 cup dry quinoa
5 cloves fresh garlic, minced
1 cup frozen or fresh corn kernels
2 tomatoes, chopped coarsely
1 cup frozen peas
1/2 cup fresh cilantro, minced
1 avocado, cut into half-inch pieces
dash of salt and pepper

Directions
Note: Rinse the quinoa seeds with water until water runs clear, prior to cooking.

In a large pan on low heat, combine bell pepper, oil, onion, and pinch of salt.

Cover and cook on medium-low until vegetables are soft. Stirring occasionally and cook for about 10 minutes.

Add paprika, coriander, cumin, and garlic.

Increase heat and stir in potatoes and broth. Bring to a boil. Then reduce heat and simmer ten minutes.

Stir in quinoa and continue simmering for 5 minutes.

Stir in corn. Simmer another 5 minutes or until potatoes and quinoa are soft.

Stir in tomatoes and peas and cook for an additional two minutes.

Remove from heat. Add avocado, cilantro and season with salt and pepper. Stir. Makes six servings.

Feta Cheese and Quinoa Patties
These patties are an excellent alternative to hamburgers. They are tasty and their consistency is much like that of a hamburger.

Ingredients
2 cups dry quinoa
5 eggs, beaten
1/2 teaspoon sea salt
1/3 cup fresh chives, chopped fine
1/3 cup fresh dill, chopped fine
1 cup kale, chopped fine

1 white onion, chopped fine
3 cloves fresh garlic, chopped fine
1 teaspoon cumin
1 teaspoon baking powder
1 cup whole grain bread crumbs
1/3 cup crumbled feta cheese
1 tablespoon clarified butter or olive oil

Directions

Note: Rinse the quinoa seeds with water until water runs clear, prior to cooking.

Preheat oven to 400 (F).

In a medium saucepan, combine quinoa with 3 cups water and 1/2 teaspoon salt.

Bring to a boil, then cover and reduce heat. Simmer until water is absorbed and quinoa is soft, about 25 minutes.

Remove from heat and cool.

In large bowl, stir together eggs, salt, and quinoa.

To the egg mixture add the kale, onion, garlic, chives, cumin, and dill. Stir well.

To the mixture stir in bread crumbs and baking powder.

Stir in feta cheese.

Mold mixture into 12 patties.

Coat a baking sheet with cooking spray and place patties.

Bake for 20 minutes.

Flip each patty over and bake an additional 5 minutes.

Yields one dozen patties.

Quinoa Treats and Desserts

Even desserts can have an extra kick of nutrition without sacrificing taste when you add quinoa.

Coconut and Blueberry Quinoa Pudding

My daughter created this one day when she was looking for a snack. Originally she just used soymilk, but we then added the coconut milk to add more flavor. It is really good!

Ingredients
1 cup dry quinoa
1 cup soymilk
1/4 cup honey
1 pint blueberries
1 1/2 cups water
1 cup coconut milk

Directions
Note: Rinse the quinoa seeds with water until water runs clear, prior to cooking.

In a medium-sized pot, over medium heat, cook quinoa with 2 cups water until tender and most of the water has been absorbed.

In a large pan, heat over medium heat, soy milk and coconut milk. Add 1/4 cup honey and stir until melted.

Turn heat down and simmer milk mixture. Add cooked quinoa and stir.

Increase heat to medium and continue cooking until mixture thickens, stirring constantly for 2 minutes.

Stir in blueberries and remove from heat.

Place in a bowl and refrigerate. Makes 4 servings.

Fruit and Quinoa Yogurt Treat

My family loves this dessert with strawberries. But it is also delicious with blueberries or raspberries.

Ingredients
1 cup dry quinoa
2 cups water
1 1/2 cups strawberries, sliced in quarters
2 cups low fat vanilla yogurt

Directions
Note: Rinse the quinoa seeds with water until water runs clear, prior to cooking.

In a medium-sized pot, bring water to a boil and add quinoa. Reduce heat, cover and simmer 15 minutes.

Refrigerate for 20 minutes to cool.

In cup or glass, layer the quinoa, yogurt, strawberries, yogurt, strawberries and yogurt.

Top with a strawberry. Makes 4 servings.

Cranberry and Cherry Quinoa Pudding

Ingredients
1 cup quinoa
2 cups boiling water
1/2 cup dried cranberries
1/2 cup dried cherries
1/2 cup unsweetened apple juice
1 teaspoon vanilla
2 bananas
1/2 teaspoon cinnamon

Directions
After rinsing quinoa in cold water, add it to boiling water.

Reduce the heat to low and cover. Simmer slowly for 5 minutes.

To the quinoa add the dried fruit and continue simmering, covered, for another 5 minutes. All liquid should be absorbed.

In a blender place the remaining ingredients and blend until smooth.

Pour blended mixture into the quinoa pan. Remove from heat and stir.

Place pudding into a bowl and refrigerate until ready to serve. Makes 6 servings.

Creamy Peanut Butter Cookies
These cookies are excellent. If you like chewy cookies, bake them for only 10 minutes. Crispier cookies should be baked 12 minutes.

Ingredients
3/4 cup dry quinoa
2 cups water
1/3 cup brown sugar
1/2 cup butter
1/2 cup peanut butter
1/2 cup honey
1 cup rice flour
1/4 teaspoon salt
1 teaspoon baking soda

Directions
Note: Rinse the quinoa seeds with water until water runs clear, prior to cooking.

In a medium-sized pot, bring water to a boil and add quinoa. Reduce heat, cover and simmer 15 minutes.

Preheat oven to 350 degrees (F).

In a medium-sized bowl, combine the brown sugar, the butter, the peanut butter and honey until creamy.

Add the remaining ingredients and mix well.

Place rounded spoonfuls of batter onto cookie sheets and bake for 10 – 12 minutes. Makes up to 2 1/2 dozen cookies.

Honey Apple Quinoa
My family prefers this dish as a snack or dessert, but it also makes an excellent breakfast dish.

Ingredients
1 cup dry quinoa
2 cups water
1 teaspoon cinnamon
1 teaspoon honey
1 apple (we prefer Granny Smith)
1 stalk rosemary

Directions
Note: Rinse the quinoa seeds with water until water runs clear, prior to cooking.

In a medium-sized pot, bring water to a boil and add quinoa. Reduce heat, cover and simmer 15 minutes.

Chop the apple into small pieces and chop rosemary coarsely.

Add rosemary, cinnamon, apple, and honey to quinoa.

This dish can be served hot or cold.

Serves 4.

Conclusion

As you can see, quinoa is very easy to incorporate into your meals, snacks and desserts. Quinoa adds nutrition and new flavors and textures to already delicious favorites and can also serve as a base for new dishes to try. It can be served warm or cold, making it also a perfect breakfast food. Because it is a high protein source, it is an excellent way to start the day. It is easy to add to meat and to soups or chowders. You can add it to an egg mixture and make an omelet. It can be added to every day, comfort food dishes such as macaroni and cheese, meatloaf, and casseroles.

And finally, quinoa is an excellent choice when people are short on time. You can prepare quinoa ahead of time so that it is immediately ready to add to your favorite dishes. Because it is low in calories, high in nutrients and very filling, it is a good addition to any diet in which good health and weight loss is the goal.

Made in the USA
Lexington, KY
03 December 2012